I am HERE! WHERE ARE YOU?

Anita Jones
& Sarah Horne

Franklin Watts
Published in paperback in Great Britain in 2018 by
The Watts Publishing Group

ISBN 978 1 4451 5162 5

Printed in Malaysia

Franklin Watts
An imprint of Hachette Children's Group
Part of The Watts Publishing Group
Carmelite House, 50 Victoria Embankment
London EC4Y 0DZ

An Hachette UK Company
www.hachette.co.uk
www.franklinwatts.co.uk

Credits:

Anna Andersson Fotografi/Shutterstock: 4-5.
Artazum/Shutterstock: 7c.
Katarzyna Bialasiewicz/Istockphoto: 5c.
Francesco Carucci/Shutterstock: 13cr.
Cheryl Casey/Shutterstock: 5t.
Marco Ciannarel/Shutterstock: 11t.
Dedi57/Shutterstock: 7t.
Doin/Shutterstock: 9t.
Ron Ellis/Shutterstock: 6-7, 8-9.

Natali Gladd/Shutterstock: 11b.
Dave Head/Shutterstock: 10-11.
Miks Mihails Ignats/Shutterstock: 11c.
Rainer Lesniewski/Shutterstock: 13cl map.
Lumokajlinioj/Shutterstock: 7b.
Paul Maguire/Shutterstock: 5b.
Andrew Mappouras/Shutterstock: 13br.
Ingo Menhard/Shutterstock: 13bl map, 13br map.
Alex Mit/Shutterstock: 24-25.

Taveesak Pansang/Shutterstock: 26-27.
Gigi Peis/Shutterstock: 13bl.
Plan-B/Shutterstock: 19.
Aaron Rutten/Shutterstock: 22-23.
Bahruz Rzayev/Shutterstock: 13cr map.
Sailorr/Shutterstock: 20-21.
Joseph Sohm/Shutterstock: 9b.
Stocker1970/Shutterstock: 13cl.
Elvis Vaughn/Shutterstock: 9c.

I am HERE!

WHERE ARE YOU?

Hello. My name is Ollie and **this is the room** that I'm in.

I am here.

4

What sort of room are you in?

5

This is the house
that the room is in
that I'm in.

6

What sort of building are you in?

I am here.

What sort of road
are you in?

9

This is the town

that the road is in,
that the house is in,
that the room is in,
that I'm in.

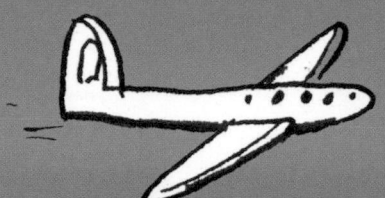

What sort of road are you in?

This is the town
that the road is in,
that the house is in,
that the room is in,
that I'm in.

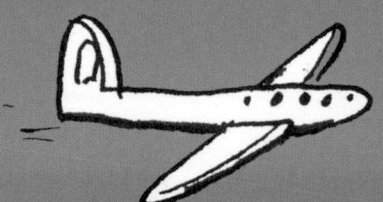

I am here.

What sort of road
are you in?

9

This is the town
that the road is in,
that the house is in,
that the room is in,
that I'm in.

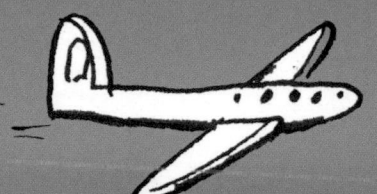

I am here.

What sort of neighbourhood are you in?

City

Town

Village

This is the county
that the town is in,
that the road is in,
that the house is in,
that the room is in,
that I'm in.

I am here.

North Yorkshire

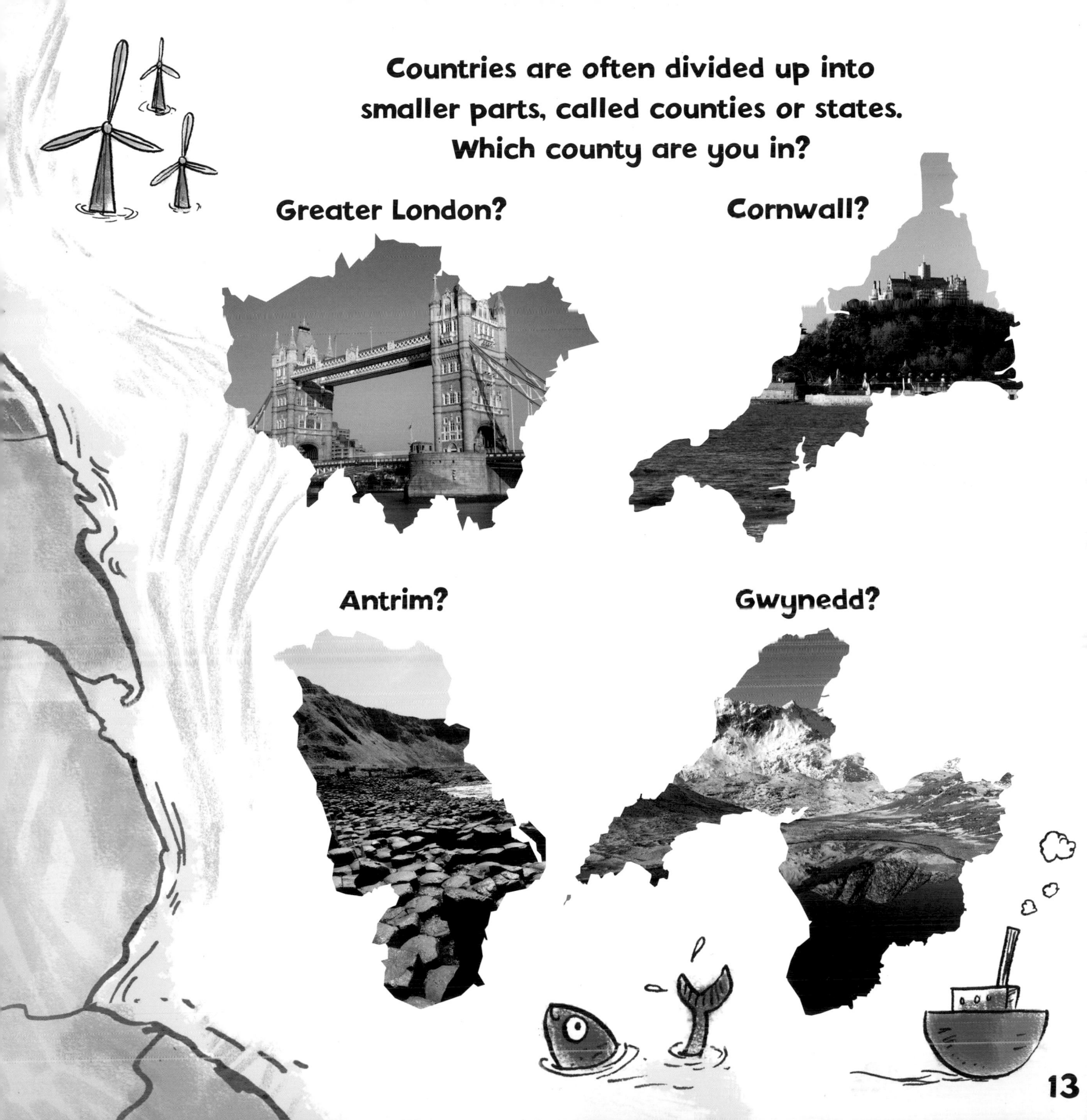

Countries are often divided up into
smaller parts, called counties or states.
Which county are you in?

Greater London?

Cornwall?

Antrim?

Gwynedd?

13

This is the country

that the county is in,

that the town is in,

that the road is in,

that the house is in,

that the room is in,

that I'm in.

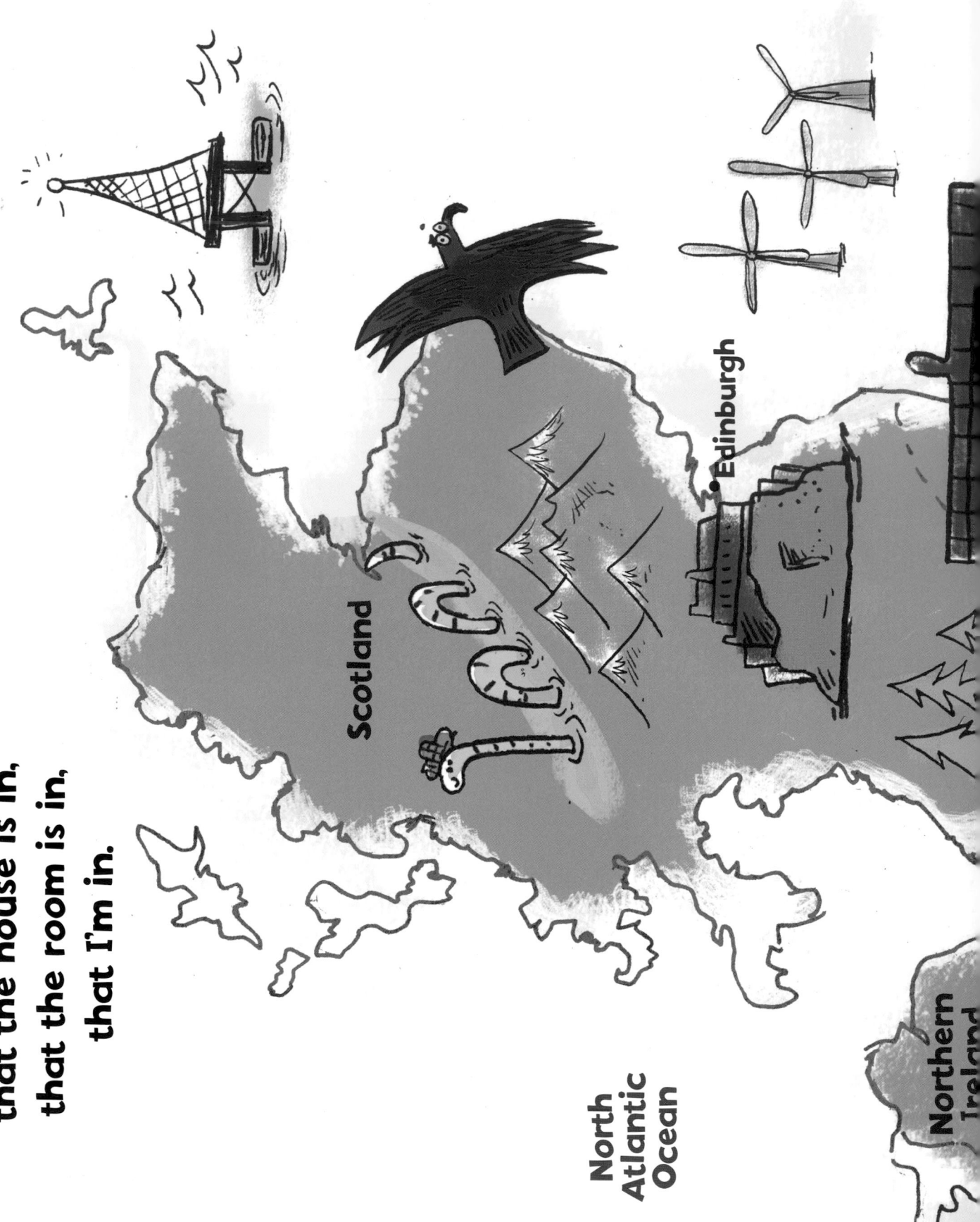

Scotland

Edinburgh

North Atlantic Ocean

Northern Ireland

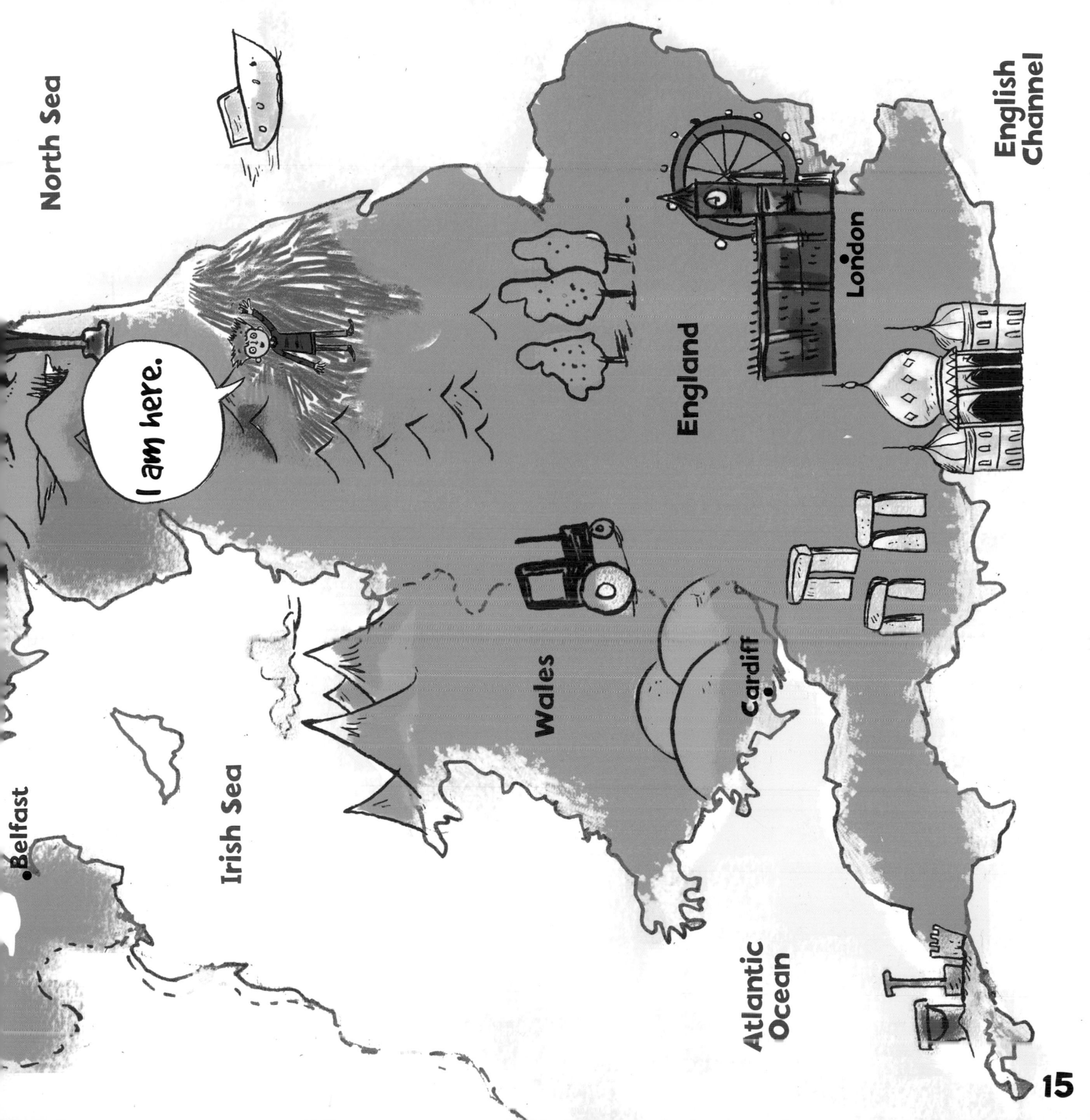

15

Greenland

Canada

North America

USA

Mexico

Atlantic Ocean

Pacific Ocean

Peru

Brazil

South America

Argentina

Which country are you in?

This is the continent

that the country is in,
that the county is in,
that the town is in,
that the road is in,
that the house is in,
that the room is in,
that I'm in.

18

Which continent are you in?

North America?

Europe?

Asia?

South America?

Africa?

Australia?

This is the planet

that the continent is in,
that the country is in,
that the county is in,
that the town is in,
that the road is in,
that the house is in,
that the room is in,
that I'm in.
Our planet is
called Earth.

This is the solar system
that the planet is in,
that the continent is in,
that the country is in,
that the county is in,
that the town is in,
that the road is in,
that the house is in,
that the room is in,
that I'm in.

Neptune

Uranus

Saturn

Jupiter

23

This is the galaxy

that the solar system is in,
that the planet is in,
that the continent is in,
that the country is in,
that the county is in,
that the town is in,
that the road is in,
that the house is in,
that the room is in,
that I'm in.
Our galaxy is called
the Milky Way.

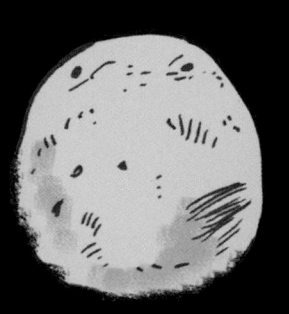

This is the universe

that the galaxy is in,
that the solar system is in,
that the planet is in,
that the continent is in,
that the country is in,
that the county is in,
that the town is in,
that the road is in,
that the house is in,
that the room is in,
that I'm in.

27

So the room that you are in is a very small part of the universe. We all live on planet Earth and we share our wonderful home with some incredible creatures.

Can you name some of them?

29

What do you think people living in that country may be doing while you are reading this book?

Here is my address:
The Street
The Town
The County
The Country
The Continent
Earth
The Milky Way
The Universe

Can you write your address like this?

Sharing this book with a child

I Am Here, Where Are You? aims to develop children's knowledge about the world, the United Kingdom and their locality. It looks to inspire curiosity about the world by zooming out from the child's immediate location to the outermost reaches of the universe.

The book is perfect for sharing, as children follow Ollie's story and have the chance to consider their own world and place within it. As you read, answer the questions posed about your own location: What sort of room are you in? What sort of road are you in? What sort of neighbourhood are you in?

Look together at the county page and explain how countries are usually divided up into smaller areas, called counties in the United Kingdom, but often called states in other countries. Look at a map of your country and find and talk about the county or state that you are in.

Next, look together at the country page – this shows the United Kingdom and the four countries that make up the United Kingdom. Point out these countries and their capital cities. Also point out the seas that surround these countries and the landmarks such as Stonehenge and the Houses of Parliament.

On the map of the world, you could discuss the different landmarks that are shown such as the pyramids, the Amazon and the Taj Mahal. Can children find the country they are in? Can they spot any other countries they might have visited on holiday?

Turn to the animal map on pages 28-29. Can children name these animals? Can they think of any animals that come from their own country? Can they think of any more animals from other countries? Discuss their favourite animals and find out how people can help to protect our world.

Finally, look at the last pages 30-31 and open a discussion about knowing people in other countries. Explain a little about time zones, and how when it is day on our side of the world, it is night on the other side of the world, so the people we know in other countries may be asleep in bed while we are working or at school. As a class activity, you could pin up a world map and ask children to invite their friends from other countries to send them a postcard – the postcards could be pinned to the world map, next to the countries they came from.

Finally ask children to write their address as Ollie has demonstrated, beginning with their road and ending with the universe.